IF MY BODY
COULD SPEAK

IF MY BODY COULD SPEAK

poems by

Blythe Baird

Published by Button Poetry / Exploding Pinecone Press

Minneapolis, MN 55403 | http://www.buttonpoetry.com

23 22 21 20 19   2 3 4 5 6

CONTENTS

You remember too much,
my mother said to me recently.

Why hold onto all that? And I said,
Where can I put it down?

—ANNE CARSON

IF MY BODY COULD SPEAK

WHEN THE FAT GIRL GETS SKINNY

the year of skinny pop and sugar-free jello cups
we guzzled vitamin water and vodka

toasting to high school and survival
complimenting each other's collarbones

trying diets we found on the internet:
menthol cigarettes, eating in front of a mirror,

donating blood

replacing meals with other practical hobbies
like making flower crowns

or fainting

wondering why I haven't had my period
in months

why breakfast tastes like
giving up

or how many more productive ways
I could have spent my time today

besides googling the calories
in the glue of a US envelope,

watching *America's Next Top Model*
like the gospel,

hunching naked over a bathroom scale shrine,
crying into an empty bowl of Cocoa Puffs

because I only feel pretty
when I'm hungry

if you are not recovering
you are dying

by the time I was sixteen, I had already experienced
being clinically overweight, underweight, and obese

as a child, *fat* was the first word
people used to describe me

which didn't offend me until
I found out it was supposed to

when I lost weight, my dad was so proud
he started carrying my before-and-after photo

in his wallet

so relieved he could stop worrying
about me getting diabetes

he saw a program on the news
about the epidemic with obesity,

says he is *just so glad* to finally see me
taking care of myself

if you develop an eating disorder
when you are already thin to begin with,

you go to the hospital

if you develop an eating disorder
when you are not thin to begin with,

you are a success story

so when I evaporated, of course
everyone congratulated me

on getting healthy

girls at school who never spoke to me before
stopped me in the hallway to ask how I did it

I say, *I am sick*
they say, *No, you are*

an inspiration

how could I not fall
in love with my illness?

with becoming the kind of silhouette
people are supposed to fall in love with?

why would I ever want to stop
being hungry

when anorexia was the most
interesting thing about me?

so, how lucky it is now,
to be boring

the way not going to the hospital
is boring

the way looking at an apple
and seeing only an apple, not sixty

or half an hour of sit-ups
is boring

my story may not be as exciting as it used
to be, but at least there is nothing left

to count

the calculator in my head
finally stopped

I used to love the feeling of drinking water
on an empty stomach

waiting for the coolness to slip all
the way down and land in the well

not obsessed with being empty
but afraid of being full

I used to take pride in being able to feel
cold in a warm room

now, I am proud I have stopped
seeking revenge on this body

this was the year of eating
when I was hungry

without punishing myself

and I know it sounds ridiculous,
but that shit is hard

when I was little,
someone asked me

what I wanted to be
when I grew up

and I said,

small

THEORIES ABOUT THE UNIVERSE

I am trying to see things in perspective.

My dog wants a bite of my peanut butter
chocolate chip bagel. I know she cannot have this,
because chocolate makes dogs very sick.
Madigan does not understand this.
She pouts and wraps herself around my leg
like a scarf, trying to convince me to give her
just a tiny bit. When I do not give in,
she eventually gives up and lays in the corner
under the piano, drooping and sad.
I hope the universe has my best interest in mind
like I have my dog's. When I want something
with my whole being, and the universe withholds it
from me, I hope the universe thinks to herself,

Silly girl. She thinks this is what she wants,
but she does not understand how it will hurt.

7

I DIDN'T ALWAYS SALIVATE OVER SKELETONS

I come over to play at my friend's house
& a chandelier of bones answers the door.
I can see each careful metal detail
of her braces poking clearly
through the skin above her top lip.
she steps on a Wii Fit balance board
& her frame is so wispy
that the system cannot detect a body.

she & I used to be fat
together.

we shared whole pans of brownies
while our mothers shared concerns
regarding our weight.
we understood the many ways
a mother's shame
can haunt a daughter's body.

an image of this friend at a waterpark
in 7th grade is still imprinted in my mind:

she jumps, jangling her arms and legs
in excitement. she looks exactly like
the flat skeletons hung during Halloween
when you yank the string at the top
of its skull, causing its glow-in-the-dark
bones to clink and clank like chimes.

for years after, this was the last moment
I can remember seeing an emaciated body

& genuinely feeling worry
instead of envy.

BEFORE THE STARVING

As a child, I invented a backyard game
called Outdoor Survival.
I snapped the necks of a dozen tulips
in my mother's garden.
I whisked daffodils into egg yolks
with sharpened sticks.
I tossed salads of lavender cabbage
& pebble croutons. I pretended to eat.

When my belly whined, I refused to
go inside. I imagined I was on an island,
living off the grid in the body of a girl
graced with the gift of not needing
to need. One night, I tried sleeping
under a heavy blanket of mulch.
I thought of Ginny Grandma's thin wrists
& whether or not it hurts to die.

Looking back, I wonder why survival
was my entertainment of choice.

Has anorexia always been
mutely boiling inside of me?

Was there a reason I mistook the sirens
of my stomach for audience applause?

I came inside only to brag,

Look, Mom!
Look how little I can get
by on!

DRESS CODE
a pantoum

Sent home.
Eleven years old.
Violation of the dress code.
Skirt: not enough. You: too much.

Eleven years old.
Beware of boys—all cave, no man.
Skirt: not enough. You: too much.
Mature prematurely. Become woman early.

Beware of boys—all cave, no man.
When you get dressed, think about the message you're trying to send.
Mature prematurely. Become woman early.
Having a body implies public property.

When you get dressed, think about the message you're trying to send.
The principal measures my hemline. Ruler to thigh.
Having a body implies public property.
How can my body say something I don't?

The principal measures my hemline. Ruler to thigh.
Violation of the dress code.
How can my body say something I don't?
Sent home.

HIGH SCHOOL

This is how to run
a stick of Chapstick down the black boxes
on your scantron so the grading machine
skips over wrong answers.
This is how to honor roll. Hell,
this is how to National Honor Society.
This is being voted *Most Likely to Marry
for Money* or *Talks the Most, Says
the Least* for senior superlatives.
This is stepping around the kids
having panic attacks in the hallway.
This is being the kid having a panic attack
in the hallway. This is making the A
with purple half-moons stamped
under both eyes. We had to try.
This is telling the ACT supervisor
you have ADHD to get extra time.
Today, the average high school student
has the same anxiety levels as the average
1950s psychiatric patient. We know
the Pythagorean theorem by heart,
but short-circuit when anyone asks us,
How are you? We don't know. We don't
know. That wasn't on the study guide.

We usually know the answer,
but rarely know ourselves.

GIRL CODE 101

We are the finaglers.
The exceptions.

The girls who have not run
the mile in four years

who layer deep V-necks
with excuses.

Eyelashes bat wiffle balls
at the male gym teachers.

We are the girls
taught to survive

by using our bodies
as Swiss army knives—

calculated scrunched nose giggles
and friendly forearm lingers

You're-so-funny-please-don't-touch-me.

We convince ourselves
there is protection in being polite

No, you can go first.
Girls: we have to be nice.

Male kindness is so alien to us
we assume it is seduction every time.

We remember age 9,
the first time we are catcalled.

12,
fraudulent bodies calling us women
before we have the chance to.

13,
the year dad says wearing short skirts in the city
is like driving without a seatbelt.

15,
we are the unmarked tardies, waived detentions,
honorable mentions in lush floral dresses.

16,
we are the public
school mannequins.

17,
we know the answer
but do not raise our hands.

Instead, we are answering
to guidance counselors who ask us

Well, what were you wearing?

Their voices:
clinkless toasts.

We are let off the hook from hall monitors,
retired football coaches who blow kisses

& whisper *Little Miss Lipstick*
into our ears in the high school cafeteria.

We shiver, but hey—at least we still get away
without wearing our student IDs!

This is not female privilege,
this is survival of the prettiest.

We are playing the first game
we learned how to.

We are the asses smacked by boys
who made welcome mats of our yoga pants.

We are easily startled.
Who wouldn't be?

We are barked at
from the street.

We are the girls petrified
by the business school boys

who learned to manifest success
by refusing to take no for an answer.

& I wonder what it says
about me

that I feel pretty in a dress
but powerful in a suit.

Misogyny has been coiled
inside of me for so long,

I forget I will not stand
before an impatient judge

with an Adam's apple,
hand grasping gavel,

ready to pound
a wooden mark.

Give me a God
I can relate to.

Commandments
from a voice both soft
and powerful.

Give me one accomplishment of Mary's
that did not involve her vagina.

Give me decisions.
A wordless wardrobe.

An opinion-
less dress.

Give me a city where my body
is not public property.

Once, my friend & I got catcalled
on Michigan avenue,

& she said *Fuck You*
while I said *Thank You*

like I was trained to.

BLOOD-ROSE
After Olivia Gatwood

the summer after 6th grade, a blood-rose blooms
  though the pleat of my crisp white bermuda shorts
while I am onstage playing The Dog Catcher
  in a local production of *Lady & The Tramp.*
mortified, I go home but at home there is no one
  to talk to about periods so I let shame eclipse
my dilemma. I am terrified to ask anyone
  in my family an uncomfortable question
so I sneak into the bathroom like a burglar
  & grab a fistful of my older sister's pads.
I taught myself to do what the women
  in my family do: ball up the wreckage of
our blood in layers & layers of toilet paper
  & bury it in bottom of the trash like a cadaver.
even then, I understood the unspoken sentiment:
  it would be gross & inappropriate for my father
or brother to ever see the messy truth of my body.
  I consulted Google & read an article that said
now, I am officially a woman & I wonder if being
  a woman has always been associated with hiding
pain. in the junior high locker room, I learn
  that the verdict is in & pads are not cool & therefore
neither am I. so I try to figure out the rocket science
  complexities of a tampon, but I am too
overwhelmed to read the instructions so I just wing it,
  which fails. I reluctantly return to stuffing
fat cotton gondolas between my thighs & then
  in sophomore year of high school spanish class,
I whisper-ask if anyone has a pad which makes
  katie & veronica gasp so I explain that tampons
don't really work for me (the one time I tried,
  deep reds still splashed my underwear like ink

& besides I heard you weren't supposed to feel it
      & I definitely felt the plastic part & it hurt).
katie said lol what do you mean the plastic part hurt?
      & veronica said ummm do you mean the applicator?
omg you do know you have to take that part off right?
      & they both frothed into giggling bubble baths
& by that they meant *how could you possibly not know this?*

BEAUTY REVELATION

Before the upperclassmen girls
with red lipstick and driver's licenses

promise to make you beautiful,

you had almost forgotten
that you weren't.

WHEN YOUR THERAPIST ASKS

blame the color pink / the sixth grade
& your sagging bib of a double chin / the plus-size
section of Limited Too / two piece swimsuits reserved
for the dandelion stem-thin girls / the time you were
the last one to finish the mile & your classmates laughed
like paper cuts, ogling your hot air balloon cheeks /
the first time you strutted downstairs in lip gloss,
kitten heels, and a short dress / your parents for choking
on their dark roasts and marching you back to your room
for becoming too much of the daughter you thought
they wanted / your lucky brother & his speechless suits /
the hours you spent watching your sister prepare
herself like a three-course meal in front of the mirror,
learning how to become appetizing / the Christmas
you unwrapped a makeup palette & saw
a tool kit / yourself for being so easy to edit / the dead
bouquet of cool, older girls you envied in the bathroom
for keeping pretty like a promise / boys who called you
beautiful but then asked if you were sick
the day you found enough courage to leave
the house without mascara / your father
for wanting to give you the same world
he is hiding you from / the year you were
the only cigarette in a carton of addicts /
your mother for not knowing how
to love a burning girl

POCKET-SIZED FEMINISM

The only other girl at the party is ranting
about feminism. The audience: a sea of rape

jokes and snapbacks and styrofoam cups
and me. They gawk at her mouth like it is

a drain clogged with too many opinions.
I shoot her an empathetic glance and say

nothing. This house is for wallpaper
women. What good is wallpaper that speaks?

I want to stand up, but if I do,
whose coffee table silence

will these boys rest their feet on?
I want to stand up, but if I do,

what if someone takes my spot?
I want to stand up, but if I do,

what if everyone notices
I have been sitting this whole time?

I am ashamed of keeping my feminism
in my pocket until it is convenient not to

like at poetry slams
or in women's studies classes.

There are days I want people to like me
more than I want to change the world.

Once, I forgave a predator because I was afraid
to start drama in our friend group.

Two weeks later, he assaulted someone else.
I am still carrying the guilt in my purse.

There are days I forget we had to invent nail polish
to change color in drugged drinks

and apps to virtually walk us home and lipstick-
shaped mace and underwear designed to prevent rape.

Once, a man on an escalator shoved his hand up my skirt
from behind and no one around me said anything

so I didn't say anything
because I didn't want to make a scene.

Once, an adult man made a necklace
out of his hands for me.

I still wake up in hot sweats
haunted with images of the herd of girls he assaulted

after I didn't report. All younger
than me. How am I to forgive myself

for doing nothing in the mouth of trauma?
Is silence not an act of violence, too?

Once, I told a boy I was powerful
and he told me to mind my own business.

Once, a boy accused me of practicing misandry.
You think you can take over the world?

And I said, *No, I just want to see it.*
I just need to know it is there for someone.

Once, my dad informed me sexism is dead
and reminded me to always carry pepper spray

in the same breath. We accept this state of constant
fear as just another component of being a girl.

We text each other when we get home safe and it does not
occur to us that not all of our guy friends have to do the same.

You could literally saw a woman in half
and it would still be called a magic trick.

That's why you invited us here, isn't it?
Because there is no show without a beautiful assistant?

We are surrounded by boys who hang up
our naked posters and fantasize about choking us

and watch movies we get murdered in.
We are the daughters of men who warned us

about the news and the missing girls on the milk carton
and the sharp edge of the world.

They begged us to be careful.
To be safe.

Then told our brothers
to go out and play.

SKIRT STEAK GIRLS

The only girl in a handful of backseat boys,
I sit shotgun without calling it.

The song pounding through the radio says
Bitch every *Bitch* other *Bitch* word.

One boy assures me I am not like other girls.
Out of habit, I thank him for the compliment.

I listen to them speak of women like menus,
medium-rare / lace skirt / trimmed steak.

I cross my legs silently & my voice becomes a jewel
in a light blue Tiffany box. I am ashamed it fits.

This is the part where I prove that I am chill.
I can hang, guys. Who says feminists are a buzzkill?

As we turn the corner, there is a gaggle
of young women. The driver of the car I am in

leans out the window & spits,
How much?

Eyes wide as stoplights, they scurry away like shot
pool balls, as I have done so many times.

The whole van hoots, fist-bumps, hollers.

There are not enough seats for both a woman
& the joke to fit comfortably in the car.

In a fish tank of predators, I worry
that I, too, am a predator by association.

When I get the courage to say something, I am
two weeks late, encouraged by Bacardi & the party.

I start by assuring him that he is a Good Person,
which is why I am telling him this in the first place.

I have to make this matter to him. I have to bring up
his sister, his mother, his girlfriend—

I have to make this all somehow
relate back to him.

It is the dilemma of the woman
who wishes to inform the misogynist

politely.

It is the dilemma of the woman
who wishes to be heard.

Let us give you this
reality check

with a spoonful
of sugar.

Let us make this easier for you
to hear

than it is for us
to live.

I DON'T HAVE TO FORGIVE YOU

a high school boy with a pop-star smile
          kindly offered to give me a ride home

& halfway there he pulled the car
          over & yanked my ponytail

like a leash & shoved my face into the pleat
          of his pressed khaki pants so hard

I cut my lip on the teeth of his zipper
          when the blood dribbled onto his belt

he laughed

when I felt the red glare
          of a video recording turn on

I fantasized about biting his dick
          all the way off

but I stiffened into a frozen polaroid
          of a trembling teenage girl instead

(you can't say no
          to a question you were never asked)

THE GHOST WHO STARS IN MY POETRY

once,
a thirty-
year-old
man tried

    to take
    Chicago
    away
    from me

        I left
        after he
        made
        a boneyard
        of my
        favorite
        city

            he was
            "slam
            famous"

                so my
                rape

                    became a
                    "community
                    conversation"

                        now
                        his only
                        legacy

                            is for

playing

       the
ghost
       who
stars
       in
my
       poet
ry

EVOLUTION OF HEALING

I.
Press snooze eight times. Smoke in the shower.
Shave one leg, forget the other. Throw hair in a messy
bun. Fuck it. Don't really want to wear makeup,
but also don't want to look ill. Read today's horoscope.
Try to call yourself out of school. It works sometimes,
but not this time. The football coach with gray hair
and a dome belly who the kids call Jerry Sandusky
and the adults call Lonely calls you things in the hallway
that make you bite your tongue all day. Nail biters spritz
special lemon juice on their nails to keep from chewing.
Wonder if this can be done to the roof of your unruly mouth.
When you were little, you were a brave girl, a fearless firecracker.
This year, you were nominated
Most Changed from Elementary School.

II.
When your mother kisses you on the scalp,
let her. Let your father hug you, hard. Not like
cradling an eggshell. Not anymore. Clean your bedroom.
Hang art on the walls. Delete the text messages.
Look people in the eyes again. Stop finding flashbacks
in the coat closet, the car, your purse. Buy a new purse.
Take piano lessons. Practice. Write songs.
Write about something other than him,
what he did, or the ash preceding the lava.
Focus on applying to college. Healing looks less like Chicago,
more like Minnesota. Less like poker, more like poetry.
Buy flowers for your mother. Drink pitchers of glitter.
Stop skipping class all the time. Do not say you didn't try.

Remember:

you did the best you could
in the situation you were in
with the materials you had.

CLASS CLOWN

For the 2014 senior prank,
a popular boy

suggests gang-raping
our female principal.

***

A freshman girl is asked to homecoming
with a plastic dildo attached to poster board:

*BECAUSE IF YOU SAY NO,
YOU CAN GO FUCK YOURSELF*

***

Did you really think
that shit was funny?

Even if you didn't,
did you still laugh?

***

That year, every day,
I wrote *I WANT TO
GET OUT OF HERE*

in the margins
of my algebra notes.

None of it
was a poem.

The point is,
every day
I wrote.

TOO PISSED TO BE SAD ANYMORE

I am sitting at home, voice low on the phone
with a sexual assault victims advocate.

She chirps,

*The first thing
you need to know*

*is that you are
not alone.*

I tell her, I know.

That's what I've been
trying to tell you.

FOSSILIZING TRAUMA

Not everything is a poem, Blythe,
my mother scoffs. I laugh because I am

certain everything is a poem if you catch it
in just the right light, like a crystal

but sometimes writing feels like I am turning
the ugly history of my body into stone.

I freeze violent memories into cement
statues in these poems

so they can no longer hurt me—
they can only stare at me

which isn't as bad, I guess.

CONCERNS FROM A HOT-BOXED JEEP

When the high slams the door
on her way out and we have nothing
to do with our hands,

I am worried some of
my relationships are based on
the clouds between us.

I am afraid of taking
so many smoke breaks
that I become one.

What if I never wake up
in the skin of the adult
I prayed for when I was a child?

What if who I am tomorrow
is an entirely different person
than who I am right now?

Or, worse,
what if it isn't?

How do I stop
carrying everything

that has ever
happened to me?

GAL PALS

In a sharp world,
I look for gentleness.

Senior year of high school,
a thought bounces around my head
like a pinball in an arcade game:

*what if I start being gay?   what if I start being gay?   what if I
start being gay?   what if I start being*

When the idea occurs to me, I am not
thinking about trauma. I am not thinking

about how when boys fuck me,
I am so bored that I count

the glow-in-the-dark plastic stars
freckling my ceiling. Instead, I am
replaying the memory of the time

a girl kissed me during a wild goose chase
of an evening in someone's dad's basement,

fueled by midnight & raspberry Smirnoff we snuck
inside the party with empty shampoo bottles

where we swallowed shots until
our lips felt like satin & Red Bull & nothing
stood still & everything was

funny.

THE WAY I WAS TAUGHT TO LOVE

My mother looks at me like I have grown
tentacles before her eyes, even though

I'm pretty sure I look the same as I did
five seconds ago

when she thought my suit jacket
was just "professional"

before she discovers
I am hella gay.

The first time I heard the word,
it dropped casually on the radio

in the minivan with my mom
the summer before 4th grade.

It dripped down the air conditioner so noticeably,
I couldn't help but ask if *gay* was a bad thing.

She explained, *It's not necessarily
a bad thing—it just isn't our thing.*

Years later, I am seventeen. Half daughter,
half apology, all fire and the wrong kind of love.

When my mother asks if I am gay, I tell her I am
sorry.

When she asks, *How can you possibly love something
that looks just like you do?*

I wonder how long
she has hated herself.

I convinced myself I could pick up being straight
like a sport. I just need to practice!

I just need to set my mind to it! I just need
to get my mom to want to be my mom again.

She sends me an email with the subject line
ARE YOU BEING GAY FOR ATTENTION?

I am drunk with shame for hiding this unsanitary secret
in the same closet as her clean linens.

She wants to know when I knew. I wish I could tell
her something simple, like maybe since the first day

of junior high when I sat behind Shannon Wittel
and smelled her Herbal Essences shampoo.

My mother is old enough to be my grandmother.
As a child, she would sing to me every night,

Blythe, I wished on a million stars
for you.

How could I not mistake the ceiling of her love
for the sky?

She tried to braid flowers in my hair,
asked if every friend was a boyfriend,

didn't mind if I brought home
a bruised wrist or black eye

as long as I had a prom date.

She would rather take a photo
of me wincing with a boy

than smiling with a girl.

My mother says her opinion
shouldn't mean anything to me

(because when has her opinion ever
meant anything to me?)

and besides, she is only one person
in the grand scheme of things,

so I know her opinion is not
the ocean

but even if the harbor isn't very deep,
people drown in their own bathtubs.

My mom insists she doesn't mind the glitter,
just the mess it's left all over the house.

She doesn't mind my sexuality—
just how it sticks to the furniture.

She is not angry with me,
just exhausted.

Now there is too much to clean up
before we have company.

MARRIAGE DIORAMA

She keeps her wedding ring on
for the same reason she refuses to leave

the house without makeup.
She swallows knives, then gets angry

when you make her spit them out
and don't name her magic.

She will throw a tantrum if you don't
let her call self-destruction a talent.

She glosses her lips with gasoline,
kisses the mouths of matchstick men

then complains everyone she loves
is on fire.

She takes an axe to the television set,
smiles at her lover and says, *Honey,*

isn't this grand?
Now the only thing

we have to watch
is each other.

TAXIDERMY

I learned love
as taxidermy

the careful art
of keeping alive

a dead thing

this is the part
that always hurts

to write

but how could I not
when this is my story

just as much
as it is my mother's

this is what it is to love
something sharp

to love the woman
who built you

even if she didn't do it
in all the right ways

even if the house
is still on fire

on the street
I grew up on—

she is the street
I grew up on

THE SHIP I BUILT

I am trying to sleep
on the front porch

of forgiveness

I am too young to be
this lonely

I didn't leave
the door of my love
unlocked

so you could
mistake my sadness
for a shelf

still, do not mistake
how open I am

for emptiness

I do not have room
to carry anyone's chaos
but mine

if I sink, it will be
in my own ocean

if I float, it will
be on the ship

I built myself

THE KINDEST THING SHE ALMOST DID

It was the year we woke up
holding hands like otters do.

She mentions I'd look cute with a gap,
so I stop wearing my retainer altogether.

When she tells me that she loves me
and that she has a lying problem on the same day,

I know I am completely and utterly
Fucked.

She makes me watch Star Wars with her,
and then she doesn't even watch it!

She watches me watching it
to make sure I'm reacting properly.

I read her daily horoscope to her while she gets ready
and even though she doesn't believe in it,

she at least tries to act interested in astrology
& all that other hippy-dippy-trippy shit I believe in

but can't prove. I fall in love with her
quickly, the way she wanted me to:

all skin and poem and Diet Coke, listening
to Regina Spektor on her bed while she

calls me babygirl
and plays with my hair

when I find a boy's hair in the rough drafts
of her poems, I pretend not to.

When I ask her what she loved about him,
she says, I know this is bad, but

he was so terrible to me, I never ran
out of things to write about.

I wonder if she wants a lover
or a writing prompt?

There is a certain high to hating yourself,
she told me once.

I try not point out the irony as she explains
how unhealthy our relationship is

between drags
of her cigarette.

When she takes me on a date to the same rink
she used to roller-skate at with her last love,

I do not sob. When she apologizes for the fact
he owns the only spare set of keys to her heart,

I assure her it is
no problem.

I try not to be jealous
of his sheer good fortune.

I do not hate him for becoming the flood in her backyard.

I do not hate myself for falling in love
with a drought dressed like a girl

But I do hate myself

for falling in love
with feeling loved.

Years later, she is drunk when she tells me:
loving you is the kindest thing I almost did.

And how impossible it still is: to train the heart to sit.

The last time she shouts at me,
my name foams madly at her mouth.

She tells me, I don't know how to love anyone
with my whole being and all at once, I feel

so stupid and so small as I remind her,
Well, I don't know how to not!

In an effort to get her to stay, I promise her,
I will be whatever you want me to be.

She tells me
that is the problem.

WHAT I COULDN'T EXPLAIN VIA TEXT

You were every airplane
I mistook for a star.

I was the first poem
you had written in months.

You were everything bright
and leaving. You were

the first person I mistook
for a feeling—if not love,

what was I supposed to
name this?

I still don't know how
to love someone

without swallowing them.

SMOKE

My dad smoked cigars his whole life
until he quit on my tenth birthday.

Now, nearly a decade later, I ask him
if he misses it. *No*, he tells me.

Except when I'm with my friends
playing poker like we used to

and one of them sparks up a fat one.

And I think about how easy it is
to forget how much you loved something

until someone around you has it.

AN INVITATION

I do not know how
       to ask my parents
if they will still come
       to my wedding.
I think my dad will.
       I suspect he will arrive,
awkward & teary-eyed,
       because I truly believe
he loves me more than
       he loves being right.
My mother does not
       bring up my sexuality
anymore. I think she is tired
       of arguing. She is sick
of reading about her faults
       in my poetry.
She hates my selective memory.
       She says, *You only ever*
remember the slammed doors.
       But why don't you
ever write about how I used
       to sing to you before
bed every single night?
       & she is not wrong—
I know, I know my mother
       wished on a million stars
for me & I am trying to remember
       that sometimes people
love us in ways we do not
       understand how to be
loved. Mom, if you read this,
       please consider it an invitation
to my future wedding.

Promise me that you will
be there no matter what.

One day, you will learn
how to give and receive love

like an open window

and it will feel
like summer every day

—SIERRA DeMULDER

LIPSTICK

Growing up, my mother taught me
that lipstick should be reserved

only for special occasions.

Now, I wear it all the time.
I am my own special occasion.

THE LESBIAN REEVALUATES

& if it turns out I'm not 100% gay,
who do I ask to forgive me?

Does this mean I have to wear a bra?
Cuz if so, I'm out.

I bought a beanie
for. this. shit.

What if I am to fall in love with a boy
after years of being your trademark lesbian friend?

I am trying to remind myself that
redefining my identity

does not make me a liar,
but if it does,

what National Lesbian Coalition
do I address my apology to?

Do I have to go back into the closet
if I already came out of it once?

I woke up dressed in shame in a boy's bed
after I already came out as gay, to double check.

To ask my heart if she was sure.

I used to find empowerment in labels.
Now I feel suffocated by them.

When I was 17, I revolved
my entire identity around being gay

and now I am worried
I will be the butt of your jokes.

You know, the one about the dyke
who just needed a good dick in her?

The boy's at school used to cackle at me,
asked me if they could bring popcorn to my bedroom

assuring me they didn't mind my sexuality
(as long as they could watch).

Apparently my love only counts
when you can click on it,

when you can whistle at it,
when it's entertaining for you to see it.

This is why I am terrified
to be wrong.

I am mostly gay; I love women.
Still, how ridiculous is it

that the first time I was
attracted to a boy post-coming out,

of all the things I could be afraid of,
it was *your* disapproval?

I never want to see the smirk
on everyone's faces

if I ever dare to wake up one day
like a white flag in a boy's arms

just as everyone suspected
I would.

EVERYTHING IS FLUID

your sexuality
is not
a promise

you have
to keep.

my sexuality
is not
a promise

I have
to keep.

I LOSE MY VOICE DURING SEX

the soft girl in my bed is all jewel-toned lipstick & good
intentions. she whispers *so what do you like?* into my skin

& I feel my voice shrink into a tiny pearl until it falls
to the ocean floor of my throat & this soft girl did nothing

wrong but I am still drowned in embarrassment,
my stiff voice clamps shut & hovers above the bed

like a shadow & my tongue tangles
into a tight cherry-stem knot.

I do not feel entitled to ask for what
I want, I don't know what I want,

me, the bitch who never shuts up has nothing
to say—I still struggle to speak during sex;

I cannot help but wonder, is this another
thing that trauma has taken from me?

did my rapists take my voice as a souvenir to
fossilize their fond memories of invading my body?

when the soft girl in my bed says she likes to be
choked, I instantly feel every light in my body

go out & suddenly I can time travel. I am
slingshotted back to the memory of the men

with fish hooks for fingernails
& barbed wire for hands,

how they coiled my neck like a python
how the lump in my throat clotted like

blood / how I waited so so so patiently
for it to be over / how I closed my eyes

how I cried / how I screamed / how I shrieked
how he heard me / how he was hurting me

how he was hard
this entire time

FOR THE RAPISTS WHO CALLED THEMSELVES FEMINISTS

Perhaps this body belongs
to the first time I was raped.

& I think about how fucked up it is to begin
a sentence with "the first time I was raped,"

& how when I talk to other women
about this, it almost seems like it's not even *if*
you've been assaulted but *when*.

Women have so much in common, such as loving
Zumba! Being interrupted! Experiencing violence!

& when another male friend turns out
to be a rapist

(the same male friend
who wore feminism across his chest
like a pageant sash)

I cannot help but remember
meeting him at a sexual violence prevention rally

& when another male friend who identifies as a feminist
gives himself permission to make a rape joke

& has the nerve to call it reclamatory,
never mind that his joke just validated the actions
of the silent predator sitting next to him.

Never mind that the joke just made a survivor
sitting across from him relive what was likely

the worst thing to ever happen to them
& you men who pose as activists

scratch your head, wonder why victims
are so terrified to report, while you shrug
your shoulders & make our trauma

into your victory lap, the reason you fist-bump
your friends over craft beers at the bar.

How could I expect this body to be perfect
for anything but the punchline?

& if I don't laugh, I am no longer
the cool girl,
but the one who can't take a joke.

I have run out of compassion for wolves. I have run
out of compassion for anyone who isn't outraged.

I ran,
& this stubborn body followed.

I am the opposite
of forgiveness. I am all rage
& shriek & flame.

Outside of the women's freshman dormitory
at Yale, fraternity pledges chanted:

*NO MEANS YES, YES MEANS ANAL, I FUCK
DEAD WOMEN AND FILL THEM WITH MY SEMEN*

A woman is found unconscious behind a dumpster,
pine needles matted in her hair, naked, wounded,

& assaulted by a star athlete. Meanwhile,
everyone is more concerned

with how this experience has taken away
her assailant's *appetite.*

This is not to say all men are hungry.
This is not even to say all men are hunting.

But haven't we all found the bones of a woman
stuck like leftovers between a full man's teeth?

There is a fraternity in Minnesota that paints
the stone lions outside their front door

the color of the panties of the last girl
they successfully assaulted.

You call this rape culture?
I call it this morning.

Shit, I was catcalled four times
on the way here.

If my trauma were made into an art
museum, the most popular exhibit

would showcase portraits of every man
who has ever raped me, snarling.

The smell of his sweat on my pillowcase follows me
to sociology & the whole class can tell

most days, I am more victim
than I am survivor.

In this room, I try to write a poem
about anything other than my sexual assault,
but all that comes out

is my throat
& his hands.

A few hours before one of my best friends raped me
on our college campus, we talked about astral projection.

He couldn't understand why I wanted
to experience it so badly. He laughed,

Why would anyone want to leave their body?

BALANCING

I am trying
to be happy

& pay attention
to the world
around me

I do not
know if it is
possible

to do both
at the same
time

THE AESTHETIC OF RAPE CULTURE

he wants you to come over to "netflix & chill," even though you
know his personal agenda involves neither Netflix *nor* chill / he wants
to communicate with you exclusively via Tinder or Snapchat / he
wants to play truth or dare / he rolls his eyes when you do not pick
dare / he believes his loneliness is your responsibility / you tell him
you're doing homework so he sends you an unsolicited dick pic and
says "haha, then what" winky face (he knows that the winky face is
#crucial) / he won't waste a single opportunity to request nudes / you
tell him your hamster died and he's all *aw babe send me a naked pic
of u pouting* / he makes you sit in polite silence and watch him play
video games / he calls you everything but your name / he doesn't give
a fuck about the best part of your day / he hates how you look in that
dress / he barks at you in the middle of Target because he doesn't get
the point of high-waisted shorts / he wants you to stop wearing
lipstick / he says you look like a pale clown / you decide to stop
wearing lipstick / you tell yourself that you didn't even like lipstick
anyway / he makes you feel smaller every day / he always wants you
to have another shot / he thinks you are the prettiest when you're
fucked up / he mistakes your alcohol poisoning for a perfect
opportunity / he pretends not to notice the way your head swings
down like a limp bird with a broken neck / the word no is not in his
vocabulary / he is most in love with you when you are drunk or silent
or both / the only thing he gave you that he doesn't take with him
when he leaves is the handprint-shaped bruises blooming like
sunflowers up your thighs / he blocks the door / he yanks your arm
like a leash when you question him in front of his friends / he makes
you apologize to the back of his hand / he pushes you against the wall
as if pinning the wings of a dead moth to cork / he presses your voice
like a crushed tulip between the pages of his temper / you are silent
and he is finally pleased with you / he is the reason you didn't get
home safe / he is the reason you spent more time in the Title IX office
last year than you did in class / he prefers to call it a mistake than call
it rape / he seems to have a lot in common with a predator / he doesn't
ever call himself a predator because he thinks that is a *strong word* /

he and everyone else like him found so much empowerment in rape
culture that it became a socially acceptable aesthetic /

irritated, he demands you explain to him
WHY ARE YOU SO AFRAID OF EVERYTHING?

and suddenly it strikes you
what a privilege it must be

to be annoyed
instead of afraid

TO LIVE IN THE BODY OF A SURVIVOR

In elementary school, everyone was hopeless-
ly possessed by a silly thing we called The Game.
It's simple: if you think about The Game,
you lose. To win The Game, you do not think
about it even if someone brings it up.
I tried to go a whole day without thinking
about it. I tried to go a whole day pretending
this body is not a memorial of violent memories.

To live in the body of a survivor
is to never be able to leave
the scene of the crime. I cannot
ignore the fact that I live here.
I have tried and failed many times.
At a leadership retreat, we play
an icebreaker activity called
Cross the Line. The instructor says,
"Cross the line if you've survived
an assault." I think to myself,

Did I survive it? Or did I just get through it?

Who is entitled to the trophy
of a survivor? I carry a bouquet
of fear, even now, even here.
I am still struck by the thunderbolt
of a predator shaped like an educator.
I have always hated The Game
because I always lose.

Sometimes, I still look
up my rapists' names on Facebook.
I consider warning the clueless women
in his photographs of the Venus flytrap

they are smiling next to, but I never do.
Sometimes, I still look up
my rapists' names on Facebook.

Perhaps this, too,
is a form of self-harm.

MORE INTERESTING THAN SUFFERING

anorexia still nips at my heels
i drooled when i saw a skeleton
i feel the fat creep up on me
but i'm trying to forget about it

i know a girl who told me recovery
is important & that healing is more
interesting than suffering i can talk
to this girl about eating disorders
but not really because when we start
talking it becomes a competition
& neither of us means for this to happen

but it does she says *i'm glad i don't eat*
xx calories a day now haha that was bad
& i can't help but think to myself oh yeah
well once i didn't eat at all for a whole week
take that i mean i hope you find healing
& i mean it i really do hope she does but
i guess i don't know if full recovery exists

because one simple comment could lure
the beast back out from my belly
& that girl i mentioned? the truth is
she keeps a scale next to her
bed so it is the first floor
her feet touch in the morning
i used to be that girl too you know

that sick girl i was really good at being
sick once i can show you pictures
do you want to see the pictures
do you want to know what happened
oh you don't want to know

what
what happened

sorry
i'm sorry
i'm all good now though i'm not *that* sick
girl anymore but i still check up on her sometimes
i still talk to her but she started it you know
i didn't mean to trigger you
did i trigger you?

IF YOUR BODY COULD SPEAK

would she
forgive you?

PRUNING INTO ART

Poetry is the way
I choose to expose

the myth
of reality

I am always trying
to be a good story

Writing is the ongoing act
of forgiving & apologizing

to the women I used
to be

I stare at myself
in the mirror for hours

as if watching
a television show

I soak in a bathtub
of my flaws

until they prune
into art

RELAPSE

Sometimes, I miss being sick.

The grimiest part of me wishes I had stayed
in that familiar city of gray and mental illness
and whatever the opposite of healing is,

where there was nothing to laugh about
but plenty to write about.

I have considered myself to be recovered
from my eating disorder for three years,
but I still write about it in present tense.

When a friend at dinner makes a casual
comment on calories, the scoreboard
in my head illuminates with numbers again.

For once, I don't want to write
about this. For the first time, I am embarrassed

instead of proud
of all the mad things I have done
for happiness.

Once, I cut a ribbon the size I wanted to be
and wore it around my waist like a bracelet.

Bathroom scales make me feel
nostalgic.

Like a scrapbook,
I flip through snapshots of my sickness,

the suppers of tobacco smoke
and red lipstick

or how I used to pack my lunch box
with floss and teeth whitening strips.

Sometimes, I still paint my nails
when I'm hungry. I can't eat
until the polish is dry.

I don't want to go into more detail
because what if you mistake this poem
for an instruction manual?

I don't know how to talk
about the rabbit hole

without accidentally inviting you
to follow me down it.

EAT

When recovery is not all yoga mats and tea
and avocados, it is work. It is remembering
that sucking on ice cubes does not count as
supper. *Body, forgive me.* It is not healthy
to drink so much water that your body
becomes a bathtub your organs float in
like loofahs. *Body, forgive me.* Trying
to ignore the caloric calculator in my head
is like trying to ignore television subtitles
and sometimes I just can't. *Body, forgive me.*
Killing yourself slowly is still killing yourself.
Wanting to die is not the same as wanting
to come home. Recovery is hard work.
Not wanting to die is hard work. Every time
you asked if I was *full* I heard *fat*, but I am
trying so hard not to do that. I am trying
not to search for the nutrition label on the back
of a birthday candle box. I am trying not to dab
my pizza with a napkin. I am trying to stop doing
things that don't make any sense. *Body,*
forgive me. I am trying. I am trying. I am
still trying.

ON AN EMPTY STOMACH

anorexia
is not
a choice
but
recovery is
one day
after years
of starving
and gaining
and fighting
I stepped
on a scale
and suddenly
that number
didn't say
anything
about me
and that night
I ate a meal
with my family
and nothing
on my plate
said anything
about me
either
later I got
ice cream
from a truck
and I didn't
have to
make myself
earn it
you cannot
change
the world
on an empty
stomach

HOROSCOPES FOR SELF-DOUBT

Aries,
no one is entitled to your forgiveness unless you feel they've earned
it.

Taurus,
shame is a useless emotion.

Gemini,
the version of yourself you are most proud of is always accessible
within you.

Cancer,
avoid getting distracted by anything that is not love.

Leo,
turning a person into a poem will not bring them back.

Virgo,
there is no right or wrong way to heal; there is only your way.

Libra,
you deserve all of the dazzling things that are on their way to you.

Scorpio,
come back to the city it was easiest for you to breathe in.

Sagittarius,
sometimes it is lucky to care about something enough for it to hurt you.

Capricorn,
find victory in the small things: the clean plate, the answered phone
call, the brushed teeth.

Aquarius,
you do not owe your progress to anyone.

Pisces,
let go of the summer you were not capable of being the person you
wanted to be.

YET ANOTHER RAPE POEM

In response to criticism I received for writing too many poems about rape

I know you think I talk
too much.

I know you don't think
this is what a "pleasant survivor"
 is supposed to sound like.

I know you are threatened
because I am
a thunderstorm of a woman

with so much
to say.

Do you know how long it took
for me to say anything at all?

Sometimes I worry I write too much
about assault. I worry this is too ugly

of a burden to talk about. I worry I am
putting too much responsibility on you,

the listener.

But when I talk about my trauma,
I am not asking you to carry it

or relieve me from it. I am just asking
for it not to be too heavy for a conversation.

These experiences take up so much
space inside of me.

This stage is the only place
I can let this trauma live
outside of my body.

There is no socially appropriate time
or place to talk about rape.
I realized this at a party I didn't want

to be at, dizzyingly drunk. Someone asks
how I'm doing and his name spills

from my mouth into a puddle of vomit
onto the floor. I apologize and apologize and
apologize until the host says, Shoot, girl.

Is sorry the only word you know
how to say?

Suddenly, I am the embarrassed girl
crying in the bathroom at the party because

I made the mistake of speaking
about what happened to me
at what was supposed to be a happy

occasion. I am afraid
of wearing my recovery too publicly.

I have noticed people only stopped
calling me victim and started calling me survivor
when I stopped talking about it.

Now I have stopped
bringing flowers to the grave
of the teenager I used to be

back when I had orchids in my hair
and polka dots on my shoes, bubbling

over with light. I used to
refuse to wear the dress
I was assaulted in. I used to imagine it
draped in a sash of caution tape

because that dress was the only witness.
I threw the underwear away.

I didn't want to write
a statement. I didn't want to file
a report. I wanted to take a shower.

I wanted to scream MY STATEMENT
IS THAT I WOKE UP TODAY.

MY STATEMENT IS THAT I
STAYED HERE IN THIS BODY.

But every day, I find new ways
to heal: I wear the dress I was assaulted in

and I don't associate it with him
just to remind myself he does not own
a single fucking part of me.

I found a way to heal through the
poetry. This stage is the only place I could
tell my story where it wasn't
a liability I was putting
onto anyone.

This stage is where I learned
to stop hoarding my suffering.

And I could give a fuck
about a slam score—this is me
healing. This is me reclaiming

ownership over my body.
This is the only place
I have control over the narrative
where he cannot interrupt me.

Even though trauma has a way of
becoming the wallpaper of my head,

watch me drag the art
out of my suffering.

Watch me plant seeds down my spine
and bloom into a garden of poetry

from every horrible thing that has ever
happened to me, all the nights my voice
turned to cement and I couldn't say anything—

Watch me build an empire from the ashes
of everything that tried to destroy me.

HERE

When I wonder if I am doing
the right thing and if I am being

what I am supposed to be being,

she reminds me: *Little sister, the only
thing you are supposed to be is*

here. I ask her, How do I do that?

And she tells me: *You already
have. You already are.*

Will I be something?
Am I something?

And the answer comes:

already am, always was,
and I still have time

to be.

— ANIS MOJGANI

ACKNOWLEDGMENTS

This book is for the following people, who have all my love and respect:

For Sierra DeMulder. Thank you for being the first person who told me I was powerful.

For Siaara Freeman. Thank you for being the Katniss to my Prim. I adore you.

For Jessie, my sweet and goofy big sister. Thank you for teaching me to remain soft.

For my mother, who I care for so much that a knot brews in my throat when I think of her.

For my dad, the steady calm in all of my storms. For Ben, my big brother. For Just Grandma.

For Haley, my sunflower. For Nash, my moon. For both of your moms.

For Mari, my best friend. Thank you for exploring this strange and enchanting life with me.

For Chavah, Donte, Mary Beth, Ladan, Erin, Maddie, Sara, Mir, Sarah, One, Marge, Olivia G., and the Simpson House Boys. Thank you for being the stars of my most favorite memories.

For Mr. Patton, my favorite teacher. Thank you for never letting anyone be invisible around you.

For Management by Morgan. Thank you for always rooting for me.

For Chicago, Lethal Poetry, Louder Than A Bomb, and the 2014 Pink Door Writing Retreat.

For the Twin Cities, Slam Camp, and Hamline University.

For Demi Lovato, my first real crush. (If ur reading this, plz marry me)

For teenage girls.

For anyone who felt less alone because of my poetry and took the time to tell me.

Thank you to Hanif Abdurraqib for being such a compassionate editor. Thank you to Sam and Dylan for having my back since I was sixteen. Thank you to all the good folks at Button Poetry. I appreciate you all.

Finally, I'd like to thank my Ginny Grandma, the gentlest angel I've ever had the luxury of knowing.
I love you. I miss you. I hope you can see me from the clouds. I hope I'm making you proud.

PREVIOUSLY APPEARED:

Thank you to Write Bloody and Andrea Gibson for giving "Girl Code 101" its first home in the We Will Be Shelter anthology (2014).

Thank you to Banango Street Lit for publishing an earlier version of "Evolution of Healing" and Drunk in a Midnight Choir for publishing an earlier version of "When the Fat Girl Gets Skinny."

Some of the poems that appear in this book debuted in a previous collection, GIVE ME A GOD I CAN RELATE TO, published by Where Are You Press (2015).

ABOUT THE AUTHOR

Blythe Baird is a poet, youth educator, and actress. Her work has been featured by *GLAMOUR*, *The Huffington Post*, *NEDA*, *EverydayFeminism*, *TEDx*, *Mic*, and more. In 2016, she was recognized as a finalist for the EduZine Global Young Achiever Award. In 2017, she won the ADCAN short film award in Los Angeles and took first place in the Art With Impact competition. She graduated from Hamline University in 2018 with dual degrees in Creative Writing and Women's Studies. She lives in Minneapolis and is working on her next book.

OTHER BOOKS BY BUTTON POETRY

If you enjoyed this book, please consider checking out some of our others, below. Readers like you allow us to keep broadcasting and publishing. Thank you!

Neil Hilborn, *Our Numbered Days*
Hanif Willis-Abdurraqib, *The Crown Ain't Worth Much*
Olivia Gatwood, *New American Best Friend*
Donte Collins, *Autopsy*
Melissa Lozada-Oliva, *peluda*
Sabrina Benaim, *Depression & Other Magic Tricks*
William Evans, *Still Can't Do My Daughter's Hair*
Rudy Francisco, *Helium*
Guante, *A Love Song, A Death Rattle, A Battle Cry*
Rachel Wiley, *Nothing Is Okay*
Neil Hilborn, *The Future*
Phil Kaye, *Date & Time*
Andrea Gibson, *Lord of the Butterflies*

Available at buttonpoetry.com/shop and more!